SCHOLASTIC

ALPHA™

Grammar and Composition

1

AF647380

Vaishali Batra
Series editor: Anne Seaton

About ALPHA™ Grammar and Composition

Welcome to **Scholastic ALPHA™ Grammar and Composition.**

This series comprises coursebooks for classes 1 to 5 and offers an easy, engaging and meaningful way to master the skills and mechanics of English **Grammar**, **Composition** and **Comprehension**.

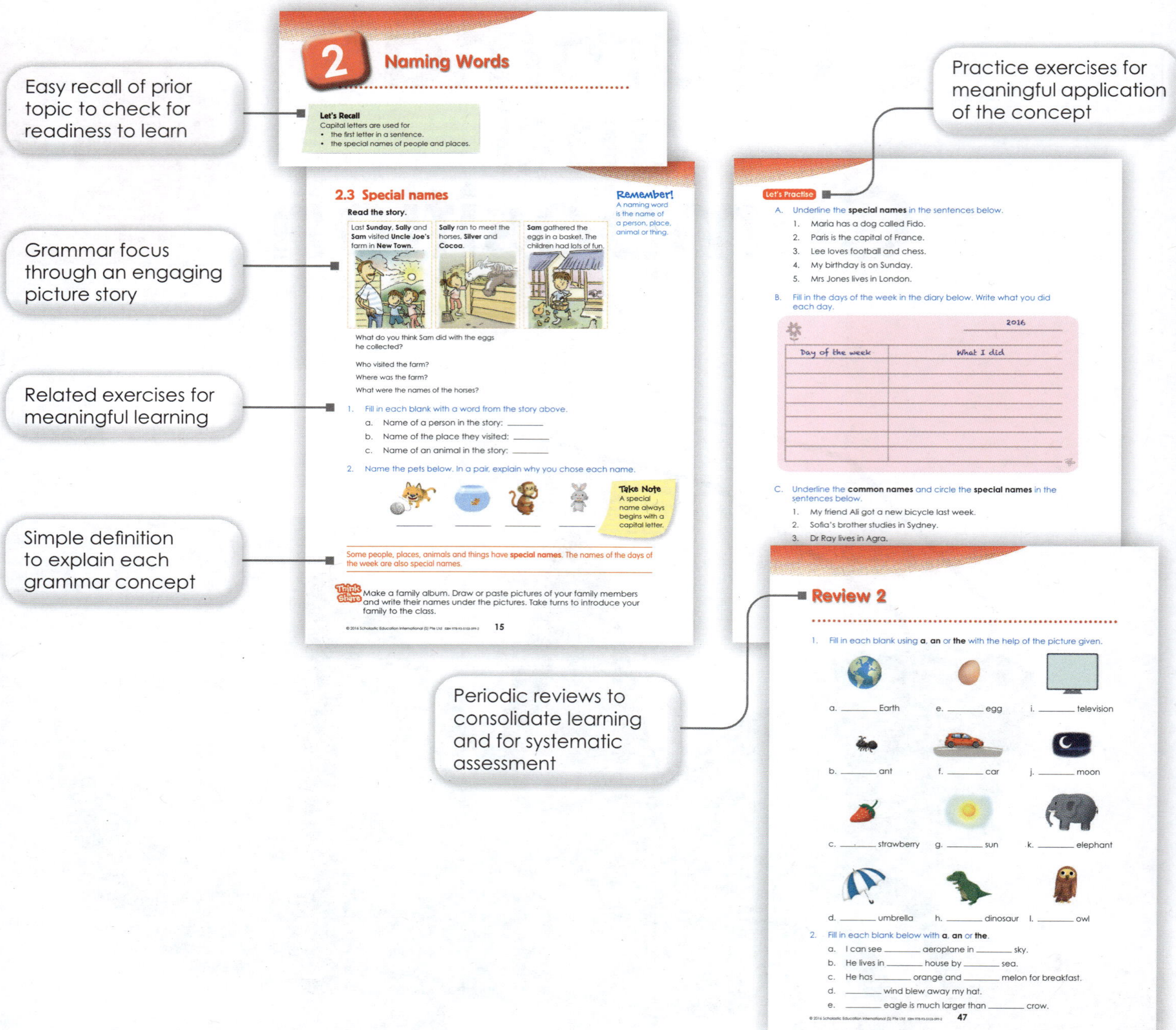

- **Take Note** provides additional tips and exceptions to rules.
- **Think & Share** activities allow opportunity for collaborative learning.
- **Remember** enhances the understanding of the concept being taught in the unit.

 ISBN 978-93-5103-599-2

Graded exercises develop key comprehension and critical thinking skills

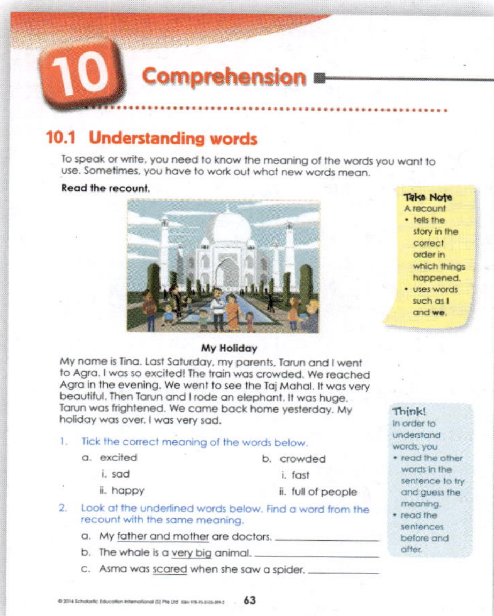
10 Comprehension

10.1 Understanding words

To speak or write, you need to know the meaning of the words you want to use. Sometimes, you have to work out what new words mean.

Read the recount.

Take Note
A recount
- tells the story in the correct order in which things happened.
- uses words such as I and **we**.

My Holiday

My name is Tina. Last Saturday, my parents, Tarun and I went to Agra. I was so excited! The train was crowded. We reached Agra in the evening. We went to see the Taj Mahal. It was very beautiful. Then Tarun and I rode an elephant. It was huge. Tarun was frightened. We came back home yesterday. My holiday was over. I was very sad.

Think!
In order to understand words, you
- read the other words in the sentence to try and guess the meaning.
- read the sentences before and after.

1. Tick the correct meaning of the words below.
   a. excited
      i. sad
      ii. happy
   b. crowded
      i. fast
      ii. full of people
2. Look at the underlined words below. Find a word from the recount with the same meaning.
   a. My father and mother are doctors. ______
   b. The whale is a very big animal. ______
   c. Asma was scared when she saw a spider. ______

63

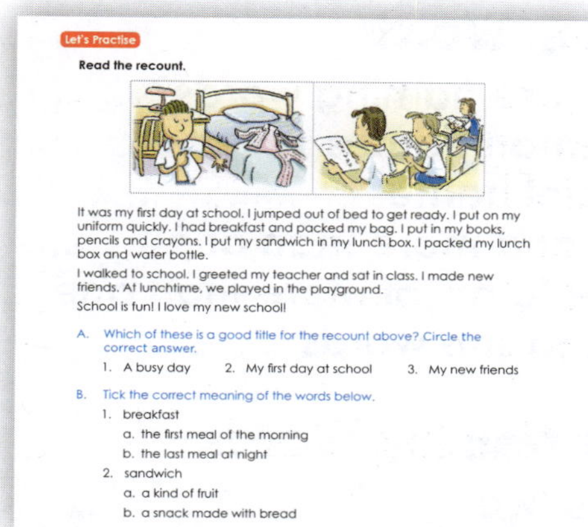
Let's Practise

Read the recount.

It was my first day at school. I jumped out of bed to get ready. I put on my uniform quickly. I had breakfast and packed my bag. I put in my books, pencils and crayons. I put my sandwich in my lunch box. I packed my lunch box and water bottle.

I walked to school. I greeted my teacher and sat in class. I made new friends. At lunchtime, we played in the playground.

School is fun! I love my new school!

A. Which of these is a good title for the recount above? Circle the correct answer.
   1. A busy day 2. My first day at school 3. My new friends
B. Tick the correct meaning of the words below.
   1. breakfast
      a. the first meal of the morning
      b. the last meal at night
   2. sandwich
      a. a kind of fruit
      b. a snack made with bread

Scaffolded exercises to develop key writing skills across varied genres and topics

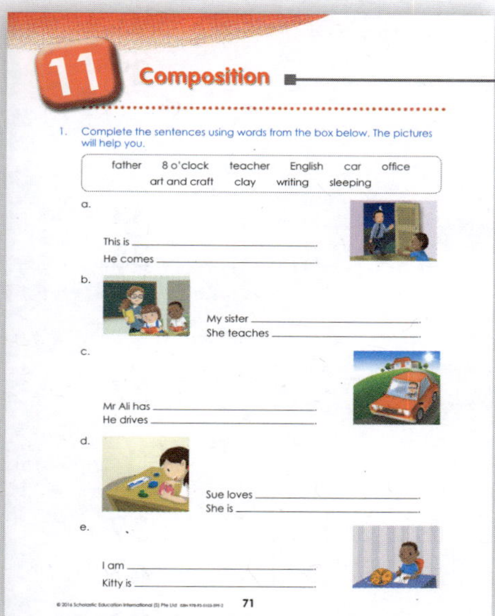
11 Composition

1. Complete the sentences using words from the box below. The pictures will help you.

father 8 o'clock teacher English car office
art and craft clay writing sleeping

a. This is ______
   He comes ______
b. My sister ______
   She teaches ______
c. Mr Ali has ______
   He drives ______
d. Sue loves ______
   She is ______
e. I am ______
   Kitty is ______

71

4. Look at the picture and answer the questions below. The words in the box will help you.

swimming flying beach reading four
bird book tree sand flower

a. What is this place? ______
b. What are Dad and the girl doing? ______
c. How many people are swimming? ______
d. What can you see on the tree? ______
e. What is the girl on the mat doing? ______

10. Write five sentences about the picture below. You may use the words in the box.

tell draw elephant classroom wrong spelling green

Vocabulary building through engaging exercises

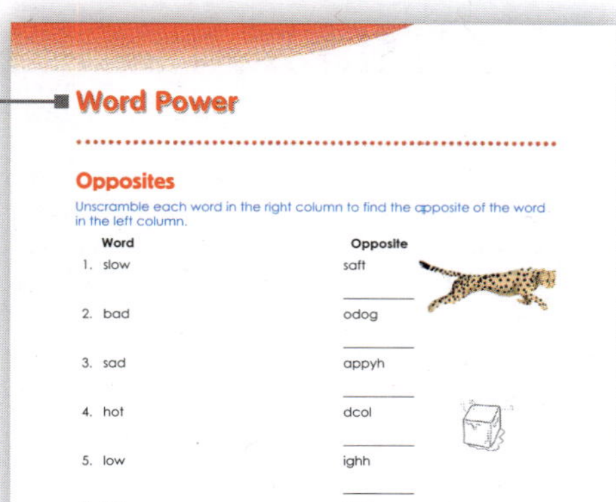
Word Power

Opposites

Unscramble each word in the right column to find the opposite of the word in the left column.

Word	Opposite
1. slow	soft
2. bad	odog
3. sad	appyh
4. hot	dcol
5. low	ighh
6. big	almls

Animal calls

What sound does each animal make? Fill in each blank with the correct word from the box below.

1. ______ 6. ______
2. ______ 7. ______
3. ______ 8. ______
4. ______ 9. ______
5. ______ 10. ______

 ISBN 978-93-5103-599-2

Contents

 ISBN 978-93-5103-599-2

8 Joining Words

9 Sentences

10 Comprehension

Word Power

 ISBN 978-93-5103-599-2

1 The Alphabet

Let's Recall
- There are 26 letters in the English alphabet.
- Each letter of the alphabet makes a different sound.

1.1 Alphabetical order

Read the story.

"Children, please line up in order," said Miss Jones.

Amina stood first in line. **B**obby stood in front of **C**indy and **D**anish.

"**Z**ayn, you are in the wrong place," said **V**iolet. "**Y**uri should stand behind me."

Why do you think Violet says Yuri should stand behind her?

In the story, who was first in line?

Who was behind her?

Who stood fourth in line?

1. Fill in each blank with the correct letter from the story above.
   a. Name of the person behind Bobby: __ indy
   b. Name of the person who should be behind Violet: __ uri
   c. Name of the person who should be last in line: __ ayn

2. Fill in the missing letters of the alphabet below.

A	B	C	D		F	G	H	I		K	L	M
N	O	P		R	S	T	U		W	X		Z

The English alphabet starts with the letter **A**. It ends with the letter **Z**. The letters of the alphabet have a fixed order called **alphabetical order**.

 ISBN 978-93-5103-599-2

Let's Practise

A. Fill in the missing letters below in **alphabetical order** to help the puppy find its bone.

B. Name the pictures below.

1. ________ 2. ________ 3. ________ 4. ________

C. Write the names of the pictures above in **alphabetical order** in the blanks.

1. ________ 3. ________

2. ________ 4. ________

D. Arrange the words below in **alphabetical order**.

1. pink, skirt, long, favourite ________________________
2. spider, hairy, big, grey ________________________
3. red, juicy, large, watermelon ________________________
4. leather, brown, dusty, shoes ________________________
5. red, umbrella, new, striped ________________________

Take Note
When we use the term **alphabet**, we mean the entire set of 26 letters. When we want to refer to particular letters, we say **letters of the alphabet**, not alphabets.

 ISBN 978-93-5103-599-2

1.2 Capital and small letters

Read the story.

What is your name?

What is your favourite sport?

Who was the surprise visitor?

Whose class did he come to?

Who loves cricket?

1. Fill in each blank with a word from the story above.
   a. Name of the day of the week: ________
   b. Name of the new teacher: ________
   c. Name of the place Grace is from: ________

2. Circle the odd one in each row below.

Take Note
- The initials in a person's name are written in capital letters, e.g. **A A** Milne, **R K** Narayan.
- The first letter in a sentence is also a capital letter.

Names of particular people, places and days of the week start with a **capital letter**. When we talk about ourselves, we use the capital letter **I**. All other letters are **small letters**.

Think & Share Make a group of four. Say three things about yourself or your family. Clap each time you use a word that starts with a capital letter.

 ISBN 978-93-5103-599-2

1.3 Vowels

1. Fill in each blank with the help of the picture given.

a. 

b__y

c. 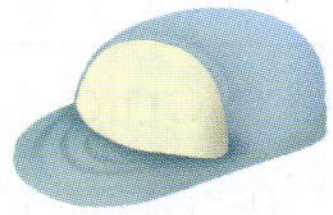

c__p

e. 

__range

g. 

__nt

b. 

__gg

d. 

__ce cube

f. 

h__n

h. 

__mbrella

2. Fill in each blank with the help of the picture given.

a. 

p__n

c. 

d__ll

e. 

j__g

b. 

b__x

d. 

b__g

f. 

f__sh

The letters **a**, **e**, **i**, **o** and **u** are called **vowels**.

Think & Share Make groups of five. List all the names in your group. Count how many names begin with a vowel. Compare your list with the other groups.

 ISBN 978-93-5103-599-2

Let's Practise

> **Remember!**
> Special names of people and things begin with a capital letter. Names of the days of the week begin with a capital letter.

A. Fill in each blank with the correct word from the brackets.

1. It was bright and sunny on ________________ (sunday/Sunday) so we went for a picnic.
2. Tomorrow is my ________________ (birthday/Birthday).
3. That orange cat is called ________________ (garfield/Garfield).
4. We visit our grandparents in the ________________ (summer/Summer) every year.
5. Mr Sharma bought a red ________________ (car/Car) last month.

B. Circle the **vowels** below.

C. Match each word with a picture. Fill in the blank with a **vowel**.

1. 	•	• a. r__se	4. 	•	• d. b__rd
2. 	•	• b. j__g	5. 	•	• e. m__ngo
3. 	•	• c. k__te	6. 	•	• f. ch__rry

 ISBN 978-93-5103-599-2

2 Naming Words

Let's Recall
Capital letters are used for
- the first letter in a sentence.
- the special names of people and places.

2.1 What are naming words?

Read the story.

A **girl** was riding her **horse** across a **field**.

The **horse** jumped over a **fence**. The **girl** fell off and hurt her **arm**.

Her **mother** took her to the **hospital**.

What do you think happened at the hospital?

Who is the story about?

What was the girl riding?

What was hurt?

Where did her mother take her?

1. Fill in each blank with a word from the story above.

   a. A person: ________
   b. An animal: ________
   c. A thing: ________
   d. A place: ________

2. Fill in each blank with the correct word from the box below.

________ ________ ________ ________ ________

rabbit	baby	pen	house	man

Everything around us has a name. These names are called **naming words**.

 ISBN 978-93-5103-599-2

2.2 Common names

1. Match each naming word with a picture below.

Person

a. boy b. grandmother c. baker d. carpenter

i. 
ii. 
iii. 
iv. 

Animal

a. giraffe b. lion c. crocodile d. penguin

i. 
ii. 
iii. 
iv. 

Thing

a. bag b. boat c. hat d. box

i. 
ii. 
iii. 
iv. 

Place

a. airport b. school c. park d. swimming pool

i. 
ii. 
iii. 

iv. 

Names for people, places, animals and things are called **common names**.

 ISBN 978-93-5103-599-2

Let's Practise

A. Fill in each blank with the correct word from the box below. The picture will help you.

bird	bus	cat
guitar	car	

1. My uncle has a small orange  ________.

2. Ray washes his  ________ every morning.

3. Look at that  ________ flying in the sky!

4. My parents gave me a  ________ on my birthday.

5. We will take the  ________ when we go to the beach.

B. Underline the **naming words** in the sentences below.

1. My father is a teacher in a school.
2. There is a cat in the garden.
3. Squirrels like to eat nuts.
4. Her house is near the river.
5. My children love going to the beach.
6. The train is entering the station.

Think & Share Pair up with a classmate. Look around you. Find two words each for people, places, animals and things. Share them with your partner and then make a class list.

 ISBN 978-93-5103-599-2

C. Find all the **common names** in the picture. Group them under the correct headings below.

Person	**Place**	**Animal**	**Thing**
________	________	________	________
________	________	________	________
________	________	________	________
________	________	________	________

D. Fill in the blanks in the story with the help of the pictures given.

On Sunday, Mark and his sister Tara went to the zoo with their father and mother. They saw lions, tigers and zebras. "Look at the giraffe eating the leaves of that ________," said Tara. Next they went to see the ________. Then Mark and Tara went for a ride on the ________. After looking at all the ________, the family had a picnic lunch and went home.

 ISBN 978-93-5103-599-2

2.3 Special names

Remember!
A naming word is the name of a person, place, animal or thing.

Read the story.

Last **Sunday**, **Sally** and **Sam** visited **Uncle Joe's** farm in **New Town**.

Sally ran to meet the horses, **Silver** and **Cocoa**.

Sam gathered the eggs in a basket. The children had lots of fun.

What do you think Sam did with the eggs he collected?

Who visited the farm?

Where was the farm?

What were the names of the horses?

1. Fill in each blank with a word from the story above.
   a. Name of a person in the story: ________
   b. Name of the place they visited: ________
   c. Name of an animal in the story: ________

2. Name the pets below. In a pair, explain why you chose each name.

____

____

____

____

Take Note
A special name always begins with a capital letter.

Some people, places, animals and things have **special names**. The names of the days of the week are also special names.

Think & Share Make a family album. Draw or paste pictures of your family members and write their names under the pictures. Take turns to introduce your family to the class.

 ISBN 978-93-5103-599-2

Let's Practise

A. Underline the **special names** in the sentences below.

1. Maria has a dog called Fido.
2. Paris is the capital of France.
3. Lee loves football and chess.
4. My birthday is on Sunday.
5. Mrs Jones lives in London.

B. Fill in the days of the week in the diary below. Write what you did each day.

2016 ______

Day of the week	What I did

C. Underline the **common names** and circle the **special names** in the sentences below.

1. My friend Ali got a new bicycle last week.
2. Sofia's brother studies in Sydney.
3. Dr Ray lives in Agra.
4. My cousin Rina is a student.
5. Tim's sister Kim loves dogs and wants a puppy for her birthday.

 ISBN 978-93-5103-599-2

2.4 One and more than one

Read the story.

There are two apple **trees**. Dad, Meg and Cody pick apples from one **tree**.

Dad carries in a basket of **apples**. Meg eats an **apple**.

There are **sandwiches** for lunch. "Don't you want a **sandwich**, Meg?" asks Mum.

What do you think Meg replies to Mum? Why?

What does Dad bring in the basket?

How many people are in the story ?

What can you see on the table?

1. Fill in each blank with a word from the story above.

   a. Meg eats an ________.

   b. The basket is full of ________.

   c. There are many ________ on the table.

   d. There are two apple ________ in the garden.

2. Match each naming word with a picture.

a. 

b. 

c. 

d. 

e. 

i. trucks

ii. bird

iii. glasses

iv. boy

v. bananas

A naming word can mean **one** or **more than one**. When we mean more than one, we usually add **-s** or **-es** to the naming word.

 ISBN 978-93-5103-599-2

Let's Practise

A. Fill in each blank with the help of the picture given. Add **-s** for naming words that show more than one.

1. one  ________

2. six  ________

3. six  ________

4. one  ________

B. Fill in each blank with the help of the picture given. Add **-es** for naming words that show more than one.

1. two  ________

2. one 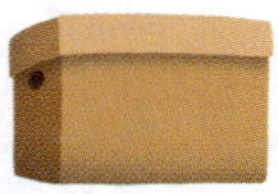 ________

3. one  ________

4. fifteen  ________

C. Fill in the blanks with the correct words from the box below. Add **-s** or **-es** where needed. The picture will help you.

sweater	storybook	dress	skirt
shoe	sock	suitcase	toothbrush

Tomorrow, Mira has a school trip. She packs her things in a ________. First she packs three pairs of ________ and two ________. She also packs a pair of black ________ and her ________. She wants to fit in her favourite green ________ and two ________. Mira also wants to carry two ________.

 ISBN 978-93-5103-599-2

2.5 Other forms of more than one

1. Match the columns below.

a. 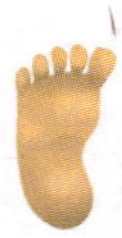	i. men
b. 	ii. foot
c. 	iii. children
d. 	iv. child
e. 	v. feet
f. 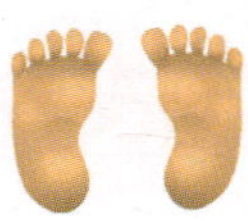	vi. man
g. 	vii. mouse
h. 	viii. mice

Sometimes we do not add **-s** or **-es** to make a naming word that means **more than one**. We use a new word to show more than one.

Think & Share Pair up with a classmate to play a "One and Many" game. Look around you and say the name of one thing. Ask your partner to change it to a word for more than one. Repeat the game after exchanging roles. Compare your lists.

 ISBN 978-93-5103-599-2

Let's Practise

A. Fill in each blank with the help of the picture given.

1. I hurt my right  ________ yesterday.

2. A  ________ climbs up the ladder.

3. Sonia has a pet  ________. It loves sunflower seeds.

4. Many  ________ play in the park every day.

B. Complete the table below with the correct word for **one** or **more than one**.

One	More than one
woman	
	teeth
child	
mouse	
	geese

C. Fill in the blanks with the correct word from the box below. Use the word for **more than one** where needed. You may use some words more than once.

mouse	woman	man	child

Two ________ and one ________ walk into a pet shop. The woman wants to buy a white ________. There are five black ________, but no white ones. The woman is unhappy. The men like black ________. They buy two black ________ for their two ________.

 ISBN 978-93-5103-599-2

2.6 He and she words

Read the story.

Father takes Tina to the hospital to meet someone.

"This is your **brother**," says **Mother**. "You are a big **sister** now!"

"We are two **boys** and two **girls** in our family now!" says Tina.

How do you think Tina feels? Why do you think so?

Who are Tina and her father visiting?

Why is she in hospital?

Why is Tina now a big sister? Is the baby a boy or a girl?

1. Fill in each blank with a word from the story above.
   - a. Tina and her ________ go to the hospital.
   - b. Tina meets her new ________.
   - c. ________ shows Tina her brother.
   - d. Tina is now a big ________.

2. Circle the correct word for each picture below.
   - a.  grandmother / grandfather
   - b.  woman / man
   - c.  lion / lioness
   - d.  peacock / peahen

Grandfather, father, brother, boy, man, lion and **peacock** are **he words**. **Grandmother, mother, sister, girl, woman, lioness** and **peahen** are **she words**.

 ISBN 978-93-5103-599-2

Let's Practise

A. Complete the table below with the correct **he** and **she words**.

He word	She word
	queen
boy	
	lioness
man	

B. Rewrite the sentences using the opposite **he** or **she word**.

1. Did you see the peacock and the lioness at the zoo?

   ____

2. My father gave this toy to my sister.

   ____

3. That boy is a prince.

   ____

4. My grandfather is older than my grandmother.

   ____

C. Look at each picture below. Make a sentence using the opposite **he** or **she word**.

1. 

____
____

2. 
____
____

3. 
____
____

Think & Share Pair up with a classmate. Tell each other about members of your family. Which **he** and **she words** do you use? List them separately. Compare your list with others.

 ISBN 978-93-5103-599-2

3 Other Naming Words

Let's Recall

- **Naming words** are names of people, places, animals and things.
- Names of particular people, places, animals and things start with a **capital letter**.

3.1 I, you, we

Read the story.

"How did **we** do in the Maths test, sir?" asks Nita.

"**You** all must try harder next time!" replies the teacher.

"How did **you** do?" asks Josh. "**I** got one sum wrong!" says Nita.

Do you think Nita is happy with her score?

Which word does Nita use to talk about her class?

Which word does Josh use in place of Nita's name?

Which word does Nita use to talk about herself?

1. Fill in each blank with a word from the story above.

   a. "Did ________ do well in the test?" Nita asked the teacher.

   b. "Have ________ got a good score?" Josh asked Nita.

   c. "________ am not happy with my score," said Nita.

2. Circle the correct word for each picture.

   a. 
   I / we

   b. 
   I / you

   c. 
   you / we

   d. 
   you / I

Some words such as **I**, **you** and **we** can take the place of naming words.

Let's Practise

A. Circle the word or set of words that best completes each sentence below. The picture will help you.

1. Sam and I are at the zoo.
   (Sam and I / We) like watching the giraffes.

2. My name is Anna.
   (Anna / I) enjoy Maths.

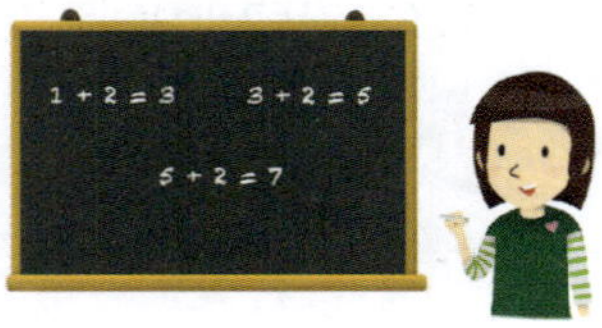

3. Hello, Molly!
   How are (Molly / you)?

Take Note
The word **you** can be used for one person or more than one person.

4. My sister and I look alike.
   (My sister and I / We) are twins.

5. Hello, Josh and Joe!
   Do (Josh and Joe / you) want to play with me?

B. Fill in each blank below with **I**, **you** or **we**.

1. Hello! My name is Mr Sharma. ________ am your new Maths teacher.
2. Raman, do ________ need any help?
3. Seema asked the children, "What do ________ want to eat?"
4. Mary and I are friends. ________ play in the park.
5. My name is Katy. ________ live in Model Town.

Think & Share Pair up with a classmate. Talk about your favourite hobby. Then ask your partner questions about his/her hobby. How many times did you use the word **I**? How many times did you use the word **we**? When did you use the word **you**?

  ISBN 978-93-5103-599-2

3.2 He, she, it, they

Read the story.

Do the people like the song?
How do you know?

Who has a big show today?

What does Alisha do at the show?

1. From the story above, match each naming word with the word used in its place.

a. Matt •	• i. she	c. people •	• iii. it
b. Alisha •	• ii. he	d. show •	• iv. they

2. Circle the correct word to complete each sentence below.

a. This is Dad. (He / She) is going to work.

b. Many people are at the bus stop. (He / They) are waiting for the bus.

c. Tina is my sister. (It / She) likes playing football.

d. Where is the book? (He / It) is on the table.

We use the words **he, she, it** and **they** in place of naming words.

ISBN 978-93-5103-599-2

Let's Practise

A. Write the correct sentence from the box to match each picture below.

It is my favourite fruit.	They like art class.	He is brushing his teeth.
It is a sunny day.	She is going to school.	

1.  ______________________________

2.  ______________________________

3.  ______________________________

4.  ______________________________

5.  ______________________________

B. Replace the underlined naming words with **he**, **she**, **it**, or **they**. Rewrite the sentences.

1. Josh is very excited because Josh is going to a wedding.

   ____

2. Mum is not well. I am making dinner so that Mum can rest.

   ____

3. The National Museum has many interesting things. Many tourists visit the National Museum every day.

   ____

4. Mr Jain is my father's best friend. Mr Jain has two pet dogs called Vicky and Rocky. Vicky and Rocky are very naughty.

   ____

   ____

Remember!

We use **I**, **you**, **we**, **he**, **she**, **it** and **they** so that we don't have to repeat the naming words.

 ISBN 978-93-5103-599-2

3.3 This, that, these, those

Read the story.

Mia sees a bracelet in a shop. "I like **that**!" she says.

Mum looks at the bracelet. "**This** costs a lot," she says.

Mia picks up a pair of earrings. "Can we buy **these**?" asks Mia. "Yes! We can buy **those**," says Mum.

How does Mia feel at the end of the story?
How does Mum feel?
Why do you think so?

Which word does Mia use in place of the word **bracelet**?

Which word does Mum use in place of the word **bracelet**?

Which word does Mum use in place of the word **earrings**?

1. From the story above, find two words used in place of each of the things below.

   a. bracelet: ________ ________

   b. earrings: ________ ________

2. Circle the correct word for each picture.

   a. 

   this / that

   c. 

   this / that

   b. 

   these / those

   d. 

   these / those

We use **this**, **that**, **these** and **those** in place of naming words.

 ISBN 978-93-5103-599-2

Let's Practise

A. Fill in each blank with the correct word from the brackets. The picture will help you.

1.  ________ is my brother sitting next to me. (This/That)

2. I have coins in my hands.  ________ belong to my dad. (Those/These)

3. 

________ is my school across the road. (This/That)

4. Look up at the lights in the sky.  ________ are stars. (Those/These)

Take Note

- We use **this** and **these** for naming words near us. We use **that** and **those** for naming words far from us.
- We use **this** and **that** for one thing or person. We use **these** and **those** for more than one thing or person.

B. Look at each underlined word. Circle the **naming word** it replaces.

1. Those shoes are too tight. These fit perfectly.
2. Which jacket is yours? This is mine.
3. There are some crayons on my desk. Are those yours?
4. What a lovely poster this is! Oh, my friend Ben gave me that.
5. Can you see the books on the top shelf? Those are Nita's.

Think & Share Pair up with a classmate. Lightly blindfold your partner and place different objects in their hand. Ask your partner to guess the names of the objects and make sentences using **this** and **these**. Then, take off the blindfold and point to objects far away. Ask them to name the objects you point to using **that** and **those**.

ISBN 978-93-5103-599-2

Review 1

1. Look at the pictures. Write the names of the children in **alphabetical order** below.

Rohan Farhan Nina Adele Kapil

____

2. Match each **capital letter** with a **small letter** below.

Y	D	M	H	B	Q	F	T
•	•	•	•	•	•	•	•
•	•	•	•	•	•	•	•
q	t	b	f	d	h	y	m

3. Circle the words that should begin with a **capital letter**.

delhi	pencil	day	cat	monday
tina	india	star	toy	thursday

4. Circle the vowel in each word below. Then replace it with another vowel to form a new word. The picture will help you.

a. p a n ________ 

b. p e t ________ 

c. j o g ________ 

d. b u g ________ 

e. c l a p ________ 

f. t o p ________ 

 ISBN 978-93-5103-599-2

5. Name the pictures. Circle the names in the word grid below.

a. 

____

b. 

____

c. 

____

d. 

____

e. 

____

f. 

____

R	E	W	T	G	H
M	I	R	R	O	R
A	R	B	E	E	A
N	E	T	E	Y	T
N	A	R	X	D	I
J	U	U	D	O	G
H	P	C	R	O	E
O	Q	K	U	N	R
P	E	N	C	I	L

6. Fill in each blank below with a **special name**.

a. Your first name __________

b. Your last name __________

c. The name of your best friend __________

d. The name of your brother or sister __________

e. The name of your school __________

f. The name of your city __________

 ISBN 978-93-5103-599-2

7. Look at the pictures in the box below. Write their names in the correct column.

One	More than one
________	________
________	________
________	________
________	________
________	________

8. Fill in the boxes with **she words** that match the **he words** below.

man ☐☐☐☐☐ king ☐☐☐☐☐

brother ☐☐☐☐☐☐ lion ☐☐☐☐☐☐☐

9. Fill in the blanks below with **I**, **you** or **we**.

Aryan: Hello Jay! Do ________ want to go to the park? ________ can play on the new slide!

Jay: ________ want to go to the park, but ________ must finish my homework first. Have ________ finished your homework?

Aryan: Yes, ________ have. I had four sums and some spelling. Do ________ have a lot of homework?

Jay: No, ________ have to study naming words. ________ can go to the park after I finish. ________ can also play on the swings.

Aryan: Yes! Have ________ played on the monkey bars? They look fun!

Jay: Yes, ________ can go to the park together!

 ISBN 978-93-5103-599-2

10. Fill in the blanks below with **he**, **she**, **it** or **they**.

This is Vikas. ________ is seven years old. His sister's name is Mansi. ________ is six years old. ________ go to the same school. ________ is a very large school. ________ has two large playgrounds and a swimming pool. Vikas and Mansi have many friends in school. In the afternoon, ________ come home with their mother. ________ live in Mysore. ________ is a city in South India. ________ is a very beautiful city.

11. Fill in each blank with the correct sentence from the box below. The picture will help you.

These are balloons.	Those are apples.	That is a car.
That is a rainbow.	That is empty.	These are dogs.
This is full.	This is a bicycle.	

Example This is an umbrella.

Those are birds.

a. 

____

____

b. 

____

____

c. 

____

____

d. 

____

____

 ISBN 978-93-5103-599-2

4 A, An and The

Let's Recall
The letters **a**, **e**, **i**, **o** and **u** are called **vowels**.

4.1 A, an

Read the story.

What do you think the birds will do next?

What do Mr and Mrs Bird build?

What does Mrs Bird lay in the nest?

What comes out of the egg?

1. Fill in each blank with a word from the story above.
   a. Mr Bird has ________ twig in his beak.
   b. Mrs Bird laid ________ egg in the nest.
   c. The birds watched as ________ chick came out of the egg.

2. Match each word with a picture.

a. 
b. 
c. 
d. 

i. a ball
ii. an ice cream
iii. a dog
iv. an orange

We use **a** or **an** to talk about one person, place, animal or thing. We use **an** before a word that begins with a vowel.

 ISBN 978-93-5103-599-2

Let's Practise

A. Fill in each blank below with **a** or **an**.

1. This is ________ book.
2. There is ________ kite flying in the sky.
3. Is ________ mosquito larger than ________ ant?
4. Do you want ________ ice cream or ________ sandwich?
5. I can see ________ eagle in the sky.
6. Mum bought ________ apple, ________ coconut and ________ watermelon.

B. Colour the correct cloud with the help of the picture given.

1. an  a

2. a  an

3. a  an

4. a  an

5. a  an

 ISBN 978-93-5103-599-2

4.2 The

Read the story.

Pitter-patter! "I can hear **the** rain," says Mum.

"Look at **the** clouds in **the** sky! **The** sun is behind them!" says Dad.

The pets are scared! "Don't worry. **The** thunder is far away!" says Mita.

Do you think Mita is worried?
Why do you think so?

What does Mum hear?

What does Dad see through the window?

What is behind the clouds?

1. Fill in each blank with a word from the story above.

a.

the ________

b.

the ________

c.

the ________

2. Fill in the blanks with the help of the picture given.

a. ________ ________ is shining.

b. ________ ________ is red.

c. ________ ________ is heavy.

d. ________ ________ is very pretty.

We use **the** to talk about a particular thing. We also use **the** before a naming word when we speak about things that are only one of their kind.

 ISBN 978-93-5103-599-2

Let's Practise

A. Fill in each blank with the correct word from the brackets.

1. ________ (a/the) sun
2. ________ (a/the) sky
3. ________ (a/the) moon
4. ________ (a/the) rain

B. Look at the pictures below. Write their names in the correct box.

A	**An**
Example cucumber	orange

C. Fill in the blanks below with **a**, **an** or **the**.

We went to the beach on Sunday. ________ sun was bright, so we sat under the shade of ________ tree. Mum, Dad and I splashed in ________ sea for some time. I had ________ ice cream. Mum had ________ apple and Dad had ________ banana. It was a wonderful day!

Think & Share Play the game "I went to the market" with your classmates. Fill up a box with cards that have the names of different kinds of food. Each student picks up a card and makes a sentence with the word given on it, for example, "I went to the market and bought an orange". The next student must add to the list without missing the names said earlier. Remember to use **a** or **an** before each word correctly.

 ISBN 978-93-5103-599-2

5 Describing Words

Let's Recall
Naming words are names of people, places, animals and things.

5.1 What are describing words?

Read the story.

Elephants are **big** animals with **white** tusks.

They can pick up **heavy** logs with their **strong** trunks.

Elephants live in **hot** grasslands and forests.

Have you ever seen an elephant? Where?

What other words can you use to talk about the elephants in the pictures?

What is the elephant's trunk like?

Where do elephants live?

1. Read the sentences in the pictures above again. Match the words that go together.

a. heavy b. big c. strong d. white

i. tusks ii. logs iii. animals iv. trunks

2. Underline the word that correctly describes each picture.

a. 

big / small ant

b. 

red / green apple

c. 

long / short hair

d. 

square / round sun

Words that tell us more about a naming word are called **describing words**.

 ISBN 978-93-5103-599-2

Let's Practise

A. Underline the **naming words** and circle the **describing words** in the sentences below.

1. The tall giraffe looks over the high fence.
2. I like eating cold ice cream on a hot day.
3. The white cat sits on a red roof.
4. Little Ziba has curly hair.
5. The large dog ran behind the brown car.

Take Note
Describing words usually come before naming words.

B. Read the sentences again. Complete the table by putting the **describing words** and **naming words** in the correct columns.

Describing word	Naming word
Example tall	giraffe

C. Colour the bubbles that have **describing words**. Match each with a **naming word**.

pretty | butterfly | dress | small | dog | big | house | golden

Think & Share Pair up with a classmate. Describe five things about your partner. Write down the describing words you use. Compare your list with your partner's and see which describing words are common to both lists.

 ISBN 978-93-5103-599-2

6 Doing Words

Let's Recall

- **Naming words** are names of people, places, animals and things.
- **Describing words** tell us more about naming words.

6.1 What are doing words?

Read the story.

It is Sports Day. The teacher **calls** my name for the race.

I **run** fast. Hurray! I **cross** the finishing line first!

I **hold** the trophy. I **smile** at the camera.

How do you think the boy feels at the start of the race?

How does he feel in the last picture?
What does the boy do in the race?
What does he do with the trophy?

1. Read the story again. Circle the word that matches each picture.

a. 

sit / cross

b. 
smile / run

c. 
call / smile

d. 
hold / hop

2. Match the animals with the way they move.

a. 

b. 

c. 

d. 

i. fly   ii. swim   iii. run   iv. crawl

Words that tell us what a person, an animal or a thing does are called **doing words**.

 ISBN 978-93-5103-599-2

Let's Practise

A. Fill in each blank with the correct **doing word** from the brackets. The picture will help you.

1. Bashir  ________ his food quickly. (cooks/eats)
2. Rima  ________ all night. (laughs/sleeps)
3. An elephant  ________ when it is hungry. (trumpets/sleeps)
4. Karim  ________ in the park every evening. (plays/reads)

B. Circle the correct **doing word** to complete each sentence below.

1. The man (read / reads) a book.
2. The frogs (hop / hops).
3. The girls (swim / swims) every evening.
4. Nitin's cat (eat / eats) fish for dinner.
5. The dolphins (jump / jumps) and (splash / splashes) in the water.

Take Note
The doing word changes when it is used for one thing and when it is used for many things, e.g.
The dog **barks** (one dog).
The dogs **bark** (many dogs).

C. Match each picture with a sentence.

1. 	• •	a. The girls smile.
2. 	• •	b. The man cleans.
3. 	• •	c. The boys laugh.
4. 	• •	d. The girl smiles.
5. 	• •	e. The men clean.
6. 	• •	f. The boy laughs.

 ISBN 978-93-5103-599-2

6.2 Is, am, are

Remember!
We use **you** for one person. We also use **you** for more than one person.

Read the story.

What do you think might happen next?

Who is Bob?

How does he feel?

How do they feel later?

1. Read the story again. Tick the correct sentence in each pair.

a. We are scared.
We is scared.

b. I are Tina.
I am Tina.

c. That is a big wave.
That are a big wave.

d. We am safe.
We are safe.

2. Match each sentence with a picture.

a. This is a dictionary. •

b. You are a good cook. •

c. I am a student. •

• i. 

• ii. 

• iii. 

The words **is**, **am** and **are** are different ways of saying **be**. We use **be** to show who we are or what something is.

 ISBN 978-93-5103-599-2

Let's Practise

A. Underline the **be word** in each sentence below.

1. I am a doctor.
2. This is my pet.
3. We are a large family.
4. Jai is my cousin.
5. You are a good cricketer.

B. Fill in each blank below with **is**, **am** or **are**.

1. The fish  ________ orange.
2. The cats  ________ in the garden.
3. He  ________ a footballer.
4. We  ________ friends.
5. I  ________ a boy.

Take Note
Am is used with **I**. **Are** is used with **you**. **Is** is used with words for one and **are** is used with words for more than one.

C. Make sentences using **is** or **are** with the help of the pictures given.

 ***Example*** These are my keys.

1.  ________________________________

2.  ________________________________

3.  ________________________________

 ISBN 978-93-5103-599-2

6.3 Is, am, are + ing

Read the story.

"The doorbell **is ringing**," says Sheila. "I **am coming**!" shouts Sam.

"What **are** you **doing**?" cries Sam. "I **am pulling** out weeds," says Sheila.

"No, you **are plucking** my lovely flowers!" says Sam.

What do you think happens next?

Why does Sam leave the garden?

What does Sheila say she is doing?

Why is Sam upset?

1. Read the story again. Circle the words in the sentences below that tell you what something or someone is doing.
   a. Sam and Sheila are working in the garden.
   b. The doorbell is ringing.
   c. I am coming.

Remember!
We use **be** to show who we are or what something is.

2. Circle the correct word to complete each sentence. The picture will help you.

a.

The birds (is / are) sitting on the branch.

c.

I (am / is) walking to school.

b.

The river (is / are) flowing.

d.

The flowers (is / are) growing.

The words **is**, **am** and **are** are sometimes used as helping words. We use them with a doing word + **ing** to show what someone or something is doing at a particular time.

 ISBN 978-93-5103-599-2

Let's Practise

A. Circle the correct **doing words** to complete the sentences below. The pictures will help you.

1. Zia (is blowing / are blowing) bubbles. 

2. The rabbits (is hopping / are hopping) across the field. 

3. I (am holding / is holding) a ball. 

4. The frogs (is sitting / are sitting) on the leaf. 

5. You (is playing / are playing) with blocks. 

B. Fill in the blanks with **am**, **is** or **are** and the correct form of the doing words given in the brackets.

It is a lovely day. The sun ________ ________ (shine) brightly. Two birds ________ ________ (build) a nest in a tree. Sofia ________ ________ (skip) in the garden. Some children ________ ________ (play) cricket in the field. A bus ________ ________ (go) down the road. Mum ________ ________ (walk) home from the market.

C. Match the two columns to make complete sentences.

1.	The moon is •	• a.	raining heavily.
2.	We are •	• b.	shining in the night sky.
3.	It is •	• c.	playing basketball.
4.	I am •	• d.	blowing hard.
5.	The wind is •	• e.	wearing a red cap.

 ISBN 978-93-5103-599-2

6.4 Has, have

Read the story.

A bicycle **has** two wheels. Some vehicles **have** more than two wheels.

This truck **has** eight wheels. A car **has** four wheels.

This boat **has** no wheels!

What other kinds of transport do you know? How many wheels do they have?

Which vehicles have two wheels?

Which vehicles have eight wheels?

Which vehicles have four wheels?

1. Fill in each blank with a word from the story above.

   a. A boat ________ no wheels.

   b. A car ________ four wheels.

   c. A bicycle ________ two wheels.

   d. A bicycle and a car ________ six wheels altogether.

   e. A truck and a car ________ more than two wheels.

2. Match each sentence with a picture.

a. Molly has curly hair.	•	•	i.	
b. The dogs have long tails.	•	•	ii.	
c. My sister has many toy cars.	•	•	iii.	
d. The elephant has a long trunk.	•	•	iv.	
e. Ladybirds have six legs.	•	•	v.	

We use the words **has** and **have** to show that something belongs to someone or something.

 ISBN 978-93-5103-599-2

Let's Practise

> **Take Note**
> When we show that something belongs to one thing or person, we use **has**, otherwise we use **have**. With **I** and **you**, we always use **have**.

A. Fill in each blank below with **has** or **have**.

1. I ________ a pet kitten. 

2. You ________ many toys. 

3. A butterfly ________ wings. 

4. We ________ many friends. 

B. Tick the correct sentences. Rewrite the incorrect sentences correctly.

1. This garden have many flowers.

____

2. My coat has three buttons.

____

3. A spider have eight legs.

____

4. I has two brothers.

____

C. Circle the correct word to complete each sentence below.

1. Lily (has / have) black hair. 

2. I (has / have) a toy aeroplane. 

3. The shop (has / have) many kinds of food. 

Think & Share Pair up with a classmate. Make two sentences about things that belong to you and to your partner using **have**. Then take turns to say two sentences about things that belong to your other classmates. When do you use **has**? When do you use **have**?

 ISBN 978-93-5103-599-2

Review 2

1. Fill in each blank using **a**, **an** or **the** with the help of the picture given.

a. ________ Earth

b. ________ ant

c. ________ strawberry

d. ________ umbrella

e. ________ egg

f. ________ car

g. ________ sun

h. ________ dinosaur

i. ________ television

j. ________ moon

k. ________ elephant

l. ________ owl

2. Fill in each blank below with **a**, **an** or **the**.

a. I can see ________ aeroplane in ________ sky.

b. He lives in ________ house by ________ sea.

c. He has ________ orange and ________ melon for breakfast.

d. ________ wind blew away my hat.

e. ________ eagle is much larger than ________ crow.

 ISBN 978-93-5103-599-2

3. Circle the correct **describing word** for each picture below.

a.  grey red brown

b.  cloudy dark bright

c.  small striped furry

d.  long square round

4. Fill in the blanks using **describing words** from the box below. The pictures will help you.

lovely	blue	green	striped
large	big	white	yellow

On Picnic Day, Mrs Joan took her class to a ________ park. The children lined up and got into a ________ bus. It was a ________ day. ________ clouds floated in the ________ sky. "Look! There is a pond beside that ________ tree," said Kaya. "Can you see the ________ frogs sitting on the lily pad?" Some children played with a ________ ball. After a picnic lunch they all went home.

 ISBN 978-93-5103-599-2

5. Circle the correct **doing word** for each picture below.

a.  brush sleep play

b.  walk eat sleep

c.  hop read walk

d.  study swim climb

e.  open talk play

f.  clean sleep walk

6. Fill in each blank below with **is**, **am** or **are**.

a. I ________ from India.

b. My parents ________ at home.

c. This ________ my homework.

d. They ________ friendly dogs.

e. I ________ hungry.

f. You ________ a good student.

 ISBN 978-93-5103-599-2

7. Fill in each blank with **is**, **am** or **are** and the correct doing word from the box below. The picture will help you.

teaching	playing	eating	flying

a. I  ____________________.

b. Geese  ____________________ in the sky.

c. Mr Mehta 

____________________ Maths.

d. The penguins  ____________________ in the water.

8. Match the two columns with the help of the pictures given.

a. She  •	• i. have an umbrella.
b. Frogs  •	• ii. have two cats.
c. The house  •	• iii. has a pen.
d. I  •	• iv. have four legs.
e. We  •	• v. has a red roof.

 ISBN 978-93-5103-599-2

7 Where Words

Let's Recall

- **Naming words** are names of people, places, animals and things.
- Words that tell us what a person, an animal or a thing does are called **doing words**.

7.1 What are where words?

Read the story.

Binny was making a burrow **in** the forest. Suddenly, he saw an eagle **above** him.

Soon, the eagle was **near** the ground. Binny was scared.

Binny quickly hid **under** a large leaf.

What do you think happens next?

Where was Binny?

Where did Binny see the eagle?

Where did he hide?

1. Fill in each blank with a word from the story above.

   a. Binny was ________ the forest.

   b. He saw an eagle ________ him.

   c. The eagle was ________ the ground.

   d. Binny hid ________ a leaf.

2. Fill in each blank with the help of the picture given.

   a. The mouse is ________ the table.

   b. The mouse is ________ the cat.

   c. The mouse is ________ the box.

Words such as **in**, **on**, **near**, **above**, **below** and **under** tell us where something or someone is. They are known as **where words**.

 ISBN 978-93-5103-599-2

Let's Practise

A. Circle the correct **where words** with the help of the picture given.

1. The books are (on / near) the shelf.
2. The train is (in / above) the ball.
3. The train is (near / below) the books.
4. The doll is (on / near) the cupboard.
5. The cat is (under / above) the cupboard!

B. Fill in the blanks using the correct **where words** from the box below. You may use some words more than once.

in	on	near	above	below	under

This is my room. There is a window ________ the bed. There is a flower vase ________ the windowsill. There are five flowers ________ the vase. There is a clock ________ my bed. My books are ________ the table. The blue and yellow books are ________ the red book. My blue suitcase is ________ the bed. My favourite teddy bear is ________ the bed.

Think & Share Pair up with a classmate to play a "where" game. Hide an object in the classroom and ask your partner to find it by asking questions. They will only be allowed to ask questions using "where words". For example, they can ask "Is it **under** the desk? **In** the cupboard? **Above** the window?"

 ISBN 978-93-5103-599-2

8 Joining Words

Let's Recall

- **Naming words** are names of people, places, animals and things.
- Words that tell us what a person, an animal or a thing does are called **doing words**.

8.1 And

Read the story.

It was Sunday **and** the parade was about to begin.

The drummers marched **and** they beat the drums.

Then the children joined in **and** the parents cheered!

Have you ever been in a parade? What did you see there?

What happened on Sunday?

What did the drummers do?

What did the parents do?

1. Read the story again. Match the sentences that go together.

a.	The children joined in. •	• i.	They beat the drums.
b.	The drummers marched. •	• ii.	The parents cheered.

2. Rewrite the pairs of sentences as one sentence below.

a. My sister went to the market. She bought apples.

____

b. Jai sees his friend across the street. He waves to him.

____

c. It is my birthday. I am going to invite all my friends to my party.

____

We use **and** to join two sentences. It is called a **joining word**.

 ISBN 978-93-5103-599-2

Let's Practise

A. Join the sentences below using **and**.

1. Tara went to the zoo. She saw a panda.

____

2. I like yellow. I also like green.

____

3. The child has apples. He also has pears.

____

4. Leila has a kitten. She also has a parrot.

____

5. I love to read books. I love to paint pictures.

____

B. Circle the word **and** in each sentence below. Then write the sentence as two separate sentences.

1. I opened the door and my father walked in.

______________________ ______________________

2. My mother is a pilot and my father is a doctor.

______________________ ______________________

3. Misha goes to the market and she buys flowers.

______________________ ______________________

4. Diya gets on the bus and it drives off.

______________________ ______________________

5. Vir puts on his shoes and he runs outside.

______________________ ______________________

 ISBN 978-93-5103-599-2

9 Sentences

Let's Recall
Words that tell us what a person, an animal or a thing does are called **doing words**.

9.1 What is a sentence?

Read the story.

We are at the museum with Miss Joy.

Miss Joy tells us about soldiers from long ago.

We see rocks dug from deep inside the Earth.

Have you ever been to a museum? What did you see there?

Who goes to the museum with the children?

What does Miss Joy tell the children?

Where did the rocks come from?

1. Underline the groups of words that make complete sense.

   a. We are at the museum. c. soldiers from long ago
   b. from deep inside the Earth d. We see rocks.

2. Rearrange each group of words below so that it makes sense.

   a. Neil name My is.  ______________________
   b. in live I Mumbai.  ______________________
   c. car a drives Suman.  ______________________

A group of words that makes complete sense is called a **sentence**. A sentence begins with a **capital letter** and usually ends with a **full stop**. It always has a doing word.

 ISBN 978-93-5103-599-2

Let's Practise

A. Write a **sentence** using the words below. The picture will help you.

1. sit butterflies flowers The on the

____

2. girl pink wearing The is a dress

____

3. school am I to going

____

4. has bananas The two monkey

____

B. Match the two columns to make **sentences** with the help of the pictures given.

1. The girl 	•	• a. in the morning.
2. This is 	•	• b. fly in the sky.
3. We exercise 	•	• c. my pet squirrel.
4. Two birds 	•	• d. has many books.

C. Tick each group of words that is a **sentence**.

1. The white owl has brown spots.
2. bakes Glenda delicious
3. Sam likes to paint pictures of animals.
4. Ostriches have long necks and long legs.
5. blue sky warm sand house red has

Remember!
A sentence always begins with a capital letter.

 ISBN 978-93-5103-599-2

9.2 What is a question?

Read the story.

"**Is there a letter for me?**" asks Mum. "Yes, this letter is for you," says Dad.

"**Who is the letter from?**" asks Dad. "It is from Uncle Jim!" says Mum.

"**What does he say?**" asks Robin. "He is coming to visit us next week!" says Mum.

Do you think Mum is happy? How can you tell?

Who brings the letter?

Who reads the letter?

Who is the letter from?

1. Tick the sentences that ask about something.

a. Is there a letter for me?

b. Who is the letter from?

c. Yes, this letter is for you.

d. What does Uncle Jim say?

2. Fill in each blank using the correct word from the box below.

How	Why	When	What

a. ________ is the colour of the book? 

b. ________ do you have dinner? 

c. ________ is Mr Gupta running? 

d. ________ many blocks do I have? 

A sentence that asks something is called a **question**. A question begins with a **capital letter** and ends with a **question mark**.

Think & Share Pair up with a classmate. Take turns to ask each other two questions. What words did you use to begin your questions?

 ISBN 978-93-5103-599-2

Let's Practise

A. Write a **question** using the words in each box below.

1. friend is best that your

____

2. answer the what is

____

3. are the party going you to

____

4. live there you do

____

Take Note
Who, **when**, **where**, **what**, **why** and **how** are called **question words**.

B. Write a **question** for each picture below.

1. ______________________________

2. ______________________________

3. ______________________________

4. ______________________________

C. Circle the **questions** and underline the **sentences** below.

1. When is your birthday?
2. The water is very cold.
3. Are you a dancer?

 ISBN 978-93-5103-599-2

Review 3

1. Fill in each blank using the correct **where word** from the box below. The picture will help you.

near	below	in	above	on	under

a. The apples are  ________ the plate.

b. The cherries are  ________ the cup.

c. My bed is  ________ the window.

d. The pink book is  ________ the orange book.

e. The children are standing  ________ the lamp post.

f. The yellow ring is 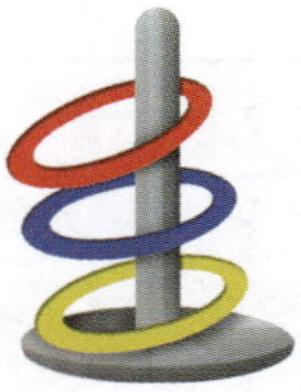 ________ the purple ring.

 ISBN 978-93-5103-599-2

2. Circle the correct **where words** with the help of the picture given.

There are three people (on / in) the tower. King John sits by the window. Princess Jeanie waves from the window (below / above) King John. Her window is (under / above) the baker's window. There is a staircase (near / under) the baker's window. Knight Ronald is (near / under) the tower. He sits (above / on) a horse.

3. Join the sentences below using **and**.

a. I have a pencil. I have a sharpener.

____

b. Anya likes to play football. She also likes to play basketball.

____

c. Turn the handle. Open the door.

____

d. Owls sleep during the day. They hunt at night.

____

e. Meera goes to the market on Sunday. She goes to the market on Thursday.

____

4. Circle the **joining word** in each sentence below. Then write the sentence as two separate sentences.

a. Look carefully and cross the road.

____

____

 ISBN 978-93-5103-599-2

b. Raj picked up a stone and he threw it into the river.

____

____

c. This book has words and it has pictures.

____

____

d. The teacher asks a question and the children answer it.

____

____

e. Mum cuts the cake and she gives me a piece.

____

____

5. Match the columns to make **questions**. The pictures will help you.

a. Who  • • i. that a duck?

b. Is  • • ii. old are you?

c. Why  • • iii. you meet me at the park?

d. Is  • • iv. teaches you Maths?

e. Will  • • v. are you running?

f. How  • • vi. this your house?

 ISBN 978-93-5103-599-2

6. Circle the sentences that ask a question and underline the sentences that do not ask a question in the story below.

Have you been to an amusement park? There are so many things to do. The roller coaster is my favourite ride. Have you been on a roller coaster? You go up and down, and round and round. My sister loves it too. Do you like ice cream? I like chocolate ice cream. My sister does not like ice cream. She likes cotton candy. I think it is too sweet! We want to go to an amusement park again. Would you like to come along?

7. Rewrite each **sentence** below using capital letters, full stops and question marks where needed.

a. i went to delhi to visit my grandfather

____

b. what is your favourite book

____

c. varun is my brother

____

d. where are my keys

____

e. my birthday is on wednesday

____

 ISBN 978-93-5103-599-2

10 Comprehension

10.1 Understanding words

To speak or write, you need to know the meaning of the words you want to use. Sometimes, you have to work out what new words mean.

Read the recount.

Take Note
A recount
- tells the story in the correct order in which things happened.
- uses words such as **I** and **we**.

My Holiday

My name is Tina. Last Saturday, my parents, Tarun and I went to Agra. I was so excited! The train was crowded. We reached Agra in the evening. We went to see the Taj Mahal. It was very beautiful. Then Tarun and I rode an elephant. It was huge. Tarun was frightened. We came back home yesterday. My holiday was over. I was very sad.

Think!
In order to understand words, you
- read the other words in the sentence to try and guess the meaning.
- read the sentences before and after.

1. Tick the correct meaning of the words below.

   a. excited
      i. sad
      ii. happy

   b. crowded
      i. fast
      ii. full of people

2. Look at the underlined words below. Find a word from the recount with the same meaning.

   a. My <u>father and mother</u> are doctors. ____________
   b. The whale is a <u>very big</u> animal. ____________
   c. Asma was <u>scared</u> when she saw a spider. ____________

 ISBN 978-93-5103-599-2

3. Find a special name from the recount to match each naming word below.

a. a girl: ______________ c. a day of the week: ______________

b. a place: ______________ d. a boy: ______________

Let's Practise

Read the recount.

It was my first day at school. I jumped out of bed to get ready. I put on my uniform quickly. I had breakfast and packed my bag. I put in my books, pencils and crayons. I put my sandwich in my lunch box. I packed my lunch box and water bottle.

I walked to school. I greeted my teacher and sat in class. I made new friends. At lunchtime, we played in the playground.

School is fun! I love my new school!

A. Which of these is a good title for the recount above? Circle the correct answer.

1. A busy day 2. My first day at school 3. My new friends

B. Tick the correct meaning of the words below.

1. breakfast
   a. the first meal of the morning
   b. the last meal at night
2. sandwich
   a. a kind of fruit
   b. a snack made with bread

C. Fill in each blank with a word from the recount above.

1. I colour my drawing with ________.
2. In my school, boys and girls wear the same ________.
3. The students ________ the principal when he walked into the classroom.

 ISBN 978-93-5103-599-2

10.2 Finding information

When you read something, you learn about it. You can answer questions by reading the text again to find information.

Look at the pictures. Read the story.

Sid's Special Day

There is a party at Sid's house. He puts on a party hat.

The doorbell rings. Sid's friends are here!
"Happy birthday, Sid!" they say.

Sid's friends stand around the table. There is a cake with pink icing. The children sing the birthday song. Sid blows out the candles. He makes a wish. Everyone gets a slice of cake!

Take Note
A picture story uses pictures and words to tell a story.

1. Tick the correct answer for the questions below.
   a. What is happening at Sid's house?
      i. a party   ii. a cricket match
   b. Which is Sid's birthday cake?
      i.    ii. 
   c. What is Sid wearing on his head?
      i. a party hat   ii. a cap
   d. What kind of birthday cake does Sid have?
      i. cake with green icing   ii. cake with pink icing

2. What does **slice** mean?
   a. piece   b. box

Think!
In order to find information, you
- read the question and underline the keywords in it.
- find the keywords in the text.
- read the information and decide on the answer.

 ISBN 978-93-5103-599-2

3. Circle the naming words and underline the doing words in each sentence.

a. The doorbell rings.

b. Sid puts on a hat.

c. Sid blows out the candles.

d. The children sing a song.

Let's Practise

Look at the picture. Read the story.

The Little Helper

Sana is a helpful girl. She wakes up in the morning as soon as the alarm rings. She makes her own bed. She feeds the cat. She brings in the newspaper and gives it to her grandfather. Then she gets dressed for school.

Sana helps her mother in the kitchen. She pours out the milk. She puts butter on her toast. She cleans up after breakfast. Then she leaves for school.

A. Read the sentences below. Write **T** for true or **F** for false.

1. Sana gets ready for bed. ________
2. Sana helps her mother in the kitchen. ________
3. Sana feeds the dog. ________
4. Sana's mother cleans up after breakfast. ________

B. Tick the correct answer for the questions below.

1. What does Sana do after she wakes up?

   a. makes her bed   b. reads the newspaper

2. What does **helpful** mean?

   a. doing things on your own   b. willing to help others

 ISBN 978-93-5103-599-2

10.3 Identifying the main idea

There are many ideas in a text, but you should try to find the one idea that joins the other ideas. This is called identifying the main idea.

Read the report.

Lions

Lions are big cats. A lion has a tan coat. A he lion has long hair around its head and neck. This is called a mane. A lion has a strong body and sharp teeth. It has a long tail with fur at the end.

A she lion is called a lioness. Baby lions are called cubs.

Lions are meat-eaters. They hunt other animals. They wait until dark to hunt.

Take Note

A report
- has a title.
- gives information about the subject.

1. What is the main idea of the report above? Tick the correct answer.
   a. How lions hunt
   b. What lions eat
   c. What lions look like and their habits

2. What is the main idea of the first paragraph?

   ____

   ____

3. Find one word from the report that means:
   a. golden-brown colour ______________
   b. long fur around an animal's neck ______________
   c. she lion ______________

Think!

In order to identify the main idea, you
- read the text and then ask yourself, "What is it mainly about?"
- look at the title. A good title often tells you what the text is about.

 ISBN 978-93-5103-599-2

4. Match each describing word with a naming word.

a. big	•	•	i. coat
b. sharp	•	•	ii. cats
c. tan	•	•	iii. tail
d. long	•	•	iv. teeth

Let's Practise

Read the report.

Baby Animals

Have you seen the babies of any animal? Some animals look the same when they grow up. Other animals change completely. A puppy grows in size when it becomes a dog. A frog looks very different when it is young.

Do you know what a young frog is called? It is called a tadpole. It looks like a tiny snake. It does not have legs. It cannot croak like a frog. A frog can jump and swim. A tadpole can only swim.

A. What is the main idea of the report above? Tick the correct answer.

1. The difference between frogs and dogs
2. The difference between frogs and tadpoles
3. How young animals look

B. What is the main idea of the second paragraph?

____

____

C. Find two questions in the report. Write them in the blanks below.

1. ______________________________
2. ______________________________

 ISBN 978-93-5103-599-2

10.4 Sequencing

To understand a text, you should work out the sequence of events, or the order in which things happen. This is called sequencing.

Read the recipe.

How to make a cheese sandwich

Things you need

1. Two slices of bread 
2. A slice of cheese 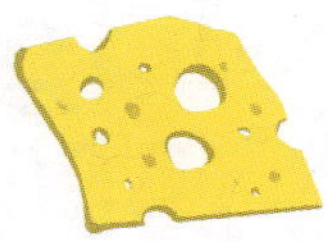
3. Butter 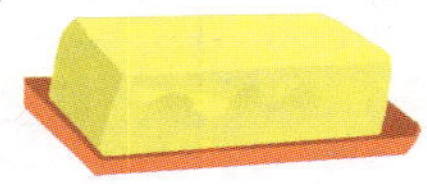
4. A knife 

What to do

1. Take two slices of bread.
2. Spread butter on one side of a slice.
3. Spread butter on one side of the second slice.
4. Place a cheese slice on the buttered side of one slice.
5. Place the buttered side of the second slice on top of the cheese.
6. Cut the sandwich in half.

Take Note

A recipe is a procedure.

A procedure

- has a heading.
- has steps in numbers that show the order in which you have to do something.

1. Number the sentences in the correct order.

   a. Place a cheese slice on the buttered side of one slice. ________

   b. Cut the sandwich in half. ________

   c. Spread butter on one side of the second slice. ________

   d. Take two slices of bread. ________

2. Circle the odd one out.

   take　　butter　　bread　　cheese　　sandwich

3. Fill in the blanks with words from the procedure above.

   a. Two doing words: ________, ________

   b. Two naming words: ________, ________

Think!

In order to work out the sequence of events, you

- find the events and underline them.
- check if the steps are numbered.

 ISBN 978-93-5103-599-2

Let's Practise

Read the procedure.

How to make an ice pop

Things you need

1. Orange juice 
2. A plastic glass 
3. A clean stick 

What to do

1. Pour orange juice into a glass.
2. Put the glass in the freezer.
3. After half an hour, put a stick in the glass.
4. Leave the glass in the freezer for one more hour.
5. Check if the juice is frozen.
6. Hold the stick and quickly pull out the ice pop.

A. Circle the correct answer to complete each sentence below.

1. The procedure has (5 / 6) steps.
2. In Step (2 / 1), you have to put the glass in the freezer.
3. In Step (4 / 5), you have to check if the juice is frozen.
4. The ice pop is (ready / not ready) in Step 3.

B. Read the sentences below. Write **T** for true or **F** for false.

1. First you put a stick in the glass. ________
2. You pull out the ice pop after the juice is frozen. ________
3. You put a stick in the glass half an hour after putting the orange juice in the freezer. ________

C. What does **frozen** mean? Tick the correct answer.

1. cold and hard
2. cold and soft

 ISBN 978-93-5103-599-2

11 Composition

1. Complete the sentences using words from the box below. The pictures will help you.

father	8 o'clock	teacher	English	car	office
art and craft	clay	writing	sleeping		

a.

This is ______________________________.

He comes ______________________________.

b.

My sister ______________________________.

She teaches ______________________________.

c.

Mr Ali has ______________________________.

He drives ______________________________.

d.

Sue loves ______________________________.

She is ______________________________.

e.

I am ______________________________.

Kitty is ______________________________.

 ISBN 978-93-5103-599-2

2. Write a sentence about each picture below. The words in the box will help you.

oranges	beads	television	family	kites

a. ____________________

____

b. ____________________

____

c. ____________________

____

d. ____________________

____

e. ____________________

____

 ISBN 978-93-5103-599-2

3. Paste a picture of your best friend and yourself. Then answer the questions below.

a. What is the name of your friend?

____

b. How old is your friend?

____

c. Where did you take this picture?

____

d. What are you doing in the picture?

____

 ISBN 978-93-5103-599-2

4. Look at the picture and answer the questions below. The words in the box will help you.

swimming	flying	beach	reading	four
bird	book	tree	sand	flower

a. What is this place? ______________________

b. What are Dad and the girl doing? ______________________

c. How many people are swimming? ______________________

d. What can you see on the tree? ______________________

e. What is the girl on the mat doing? ______________________

f. What do you see in the sky? ______________________

g. Write six sentences about the picture. You may use the words in the box.

____

____

____

____

____

____

 ISBN 978-93-5103-599-2

5. Look at the picture and answer the questions below. The words in the box will help you.

worried	mother	clinic	dog	cat
scared	checking	pet	vet	

a. What is this place? ______________________

b. Which animals can you see in the picture? ______________________

c. Who is the man in the white coat? ______________________

d. What is he doing? ______________________

e. Who is the woman? ______________________

f. How do you think the little girl feels? ______________________

g. Write six sentences about the picture. You may use the words in the box.

____

____

____

____

____

____

 ISBN 978-93-5103-599-2

6. Look at the picture and answer the questions below. The words in the box will help you.

floor	clothes	clouds	picture	
playing	home	armchair	resting	rainy

a. Where are Mum and the children? ______________________

b. What is Mum doing? ______________________

c. What are the children doing? ______________________

d. Where are the children sitting? ______________________

e. What is on the wall? ______________________

f. What do you see outside? ______________________

g. Write six sentences about the picture. You may use the words in the box.

____

____

____

____

____

____

 ISBN 978-93-5103-599-2

Review 4

1. Look at the picture. Read the story and tick the correct answer for the questions below.

Cuddles

Jaya has a cat. His name is Cuddles. Cuddles has white fur and blue eyes. His tail is soft and furry. He likes to play with wool. He runs around the room with the ball of wool. Cuddles sleeps near Jaya in a special round bed. Sometimes Jaya puts Cuddles on the windowsill. He curls up on the windowsill and goes to sleep.

a. Which word tells you that Cuddles and Jaya sleep close to each other?

   i. near ii. around

b. When does Jaya put Cuddles on the windowsill?

   i. all the time ii. some of the time

c. What shape is the bed on which Cuddles sleeps?

   i. circle ii. square

d. What does **curl up** mean?

   i. lie down in a circle ii. sit up straight

2. From the story above, find a describing word to match each naming word.

a. fur: ________ c. eyes: ________

b. tail: ________ d. bed: ________

 ISBN 978-93-5103-599-2

3. Read the sentences below. Write **T** for true or **F** for false.

a. Cuddles is a dog. ________

b. He likes to play with mice. ________

c. He has a round bed. ________

d. Cuddles has a long thin tail. ________

e. Jaya puts him on the windowsill. ________

f. Cuddles has brown fur. ________

4. Read the story and tick the correct answers below.

We visited a farm yesterday. Farmer Joe told us how he grows corn. First, he ploughs the field with his tractor. Next, he sows seeds in the field. After that, he sprinkles water on the seeds. Then, he waits for the seedlings to come out. He waters the seeds every day. Soon, the plants begin to grow. Farmer Joe always remembers to pull out the weeds. Finally, after many days, the corn turns yellow. Then, Farmer Joe cuts the corn and sends it to the market.

a. Which of these is a good title for the story?

i. At the farm   ii. Going to school

b. What is the story about?

i. How to grow a garden   ii. How to grow corn

5. Number the actions in the order that they happen in the story.

a. He waits for the seedlings to come out. ________

b. He sows seeds in the field. ________

c. The corn turns yellow. ________

d. He ploughs the field with his tractor. ________

e. He pulls out the weeds. ________

f. He cuts the corn. ________

6. Fill in each blank with a **where word** from the story above.

a. Farmer Joe sows seeds ________ the field.

b. He sprinkles water ________ the seeds.

c. The corn grows ________ the ground.

 ISBN 978-93-5103-599-2

7. Complete each sentence with the help of the picture given. The words in the box will help you.

slide	dinner	morning	play	park	home

a.  I eat ____________________.

b.  We exercise ____________________.

c.  I go to ____________________.

8. Write sentences with the help of the pictures given. The words in the box will help you.

stand	leaf	neck	clock	ladybird
	blackboard	box	giraffe	

a.  ____________________

b.  ____________________

c.  ____________________

d. 

____

 ISBN 978-93-5103-599-2

9. Look at the picture and answer the questions below. The words in the box will help you.

mouse	patting	cat	happy	dog

a. How many pets can you see in the picture? Name them.

____

____

b. What is the boy doing?

____

____

c. Do you think the children look after their pets? Why do you think so?

____

____

10. Write five sentences about the picture below. You may use the words in the box.

tell	draw	elephant	classroom	wrong	spelling	green

____

____

____

____

____

____

 ISBN 978-93-5103-599-2

Word Power

Opposites

Unscramble each word in the right column to find the opposite of the word in the left column.

	Word	Opposite
1.	slow	saft ________
2.	bad	odog ________
3.	sad	appyh ________
4.	hot	dcol ________
5.	low	ighh ________
6.	big	almls ________
7.	dry	ewt ________
8.	far	rena ________
9.	hard	tofs ________
10.	day	ghtni ________

 ISBN 978-93-5103-599-2

Same-sounding words

Some words sound the same but have different meanings and spellings.
Fill in the blanks below with the correct word.

1. You must ________ quiet when the teacher is teaching. be/bee
   The yellow ________ sits on a flower.

2. "________! I have to leave now," said Tina. bye/buy
   "Remember to ________ apples," said Mum.

3. ________ go to school by bus. eye/I
   My ________ is red.

4. You need ________ to make a cake. flower/flour
   That is a pretty ________!

5. "Sit down ________," Miss Roy said. hear/here
   "Can you ________ the bell?" asked Miss Mehta.

6. Do you ________ the answer? know/no
   ________, you cannot go out now.

7. Mili has long black ________. hare/hair
   The ________ can run very fast.

8. What is the name ________ your school? off/of
   Take ________ your shoes outside.

9. The ________ looks so blue today! sea/see
   Can you ________ the rainbow?

10. The ________ is behind the clouds. son/sun
    My uncle's ________ is my cousin.

  ISBN 978-93-5103-599-2

Rhyming words

Match each picture in Column A with a word in Column B to make a rhyming pair.

	Column A	Column B	
1.		a.	grow
2.		b.	bell
3.		c.	hair
4.		d.	tall
5.		e.	pail
6.		f.	nose
7.		g.	cook
8.		h.	coat
9.		i.	king
10.		j.	jar

 ISBN 978-93-5103-599-2

Our helpers

Do you know the people below? Fill in the blanks to find out who they are.

1. I deliver your letters. I work at the post office.

   I am a  p __ __ t __ __ n.

2. I make beautiful paintings. I use a paintbrush and colours.

   I am a  p __ __ __ t __ __.

3. I teach children. I work in a school.

   I am a  t __ __ c __ __ __.

4. I cut your hair when it grows too long. I use scissors.

   I am a  b __ __ b __ r.

5. I work in a hospital. You come to me when you are sick.

   I am a  d __ __ t __ r.

6. I drive a fire engine. I put out fires.

   I am a  f __ __ ef __ gh __ __ r.

7. I keep you safe. I chase thieves.

   I am a  p __ l __ __ __ m __ n.

 ISBN 978-93-5103-599-2

Animal homes

Help each animal find its home. Match Column A with Column B.

Column A			Column B
1. rabbit	•	•	a. hive 
2. dog	•	•	b. pond 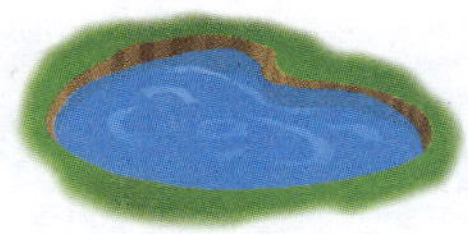
3. bird	•	•	c. den 
4. lion	•	•	d. burrow 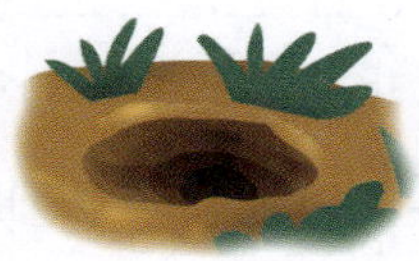
5. bee	•	•	e. shed 
6. cow	•	•	f. web 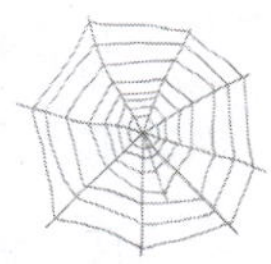
7. duck	•	•	g. nest 
8. spider	•	•	h. kennel 

 ISBN 978-93-5103-599-2

Animal calls

What sound does each animal make? Fill in each blank with the correct word from the box below.

1.  ________
2.  ________
3.  ________
4.  ________
5.  ________
6.  ________
7.  ________
8.  ________
9.  ________
10.  ________

croaks chirps mews moos chatters
quacks trumpets barks hoots roars

Animal babies

Circle the names of baby animals in the word grid below. The words in the box will help you.

F	C	A	L	F	D	W
U	A	T	R	E	E	J
P	K	I	T	T	E	N
T	F	B	O	Y	R	S
J	O	E	Y	L	K	T
E	S	E	G	I	R	O
L	K	C	O	H	C	C
M	G	U	I	R	D	H
N	I	B	T	Z	Z	I
A	C	K	E	T	S	C
P	U	P	P	Y	S	K

kitten cub chick puppy joey calf

 ISBN 978-93-5103-599-2

Colours

Look at the picture. Fill in each blank below with the correct colour.

1. ________ dress
2. ________ ball
3. ________ umbrella
4. ________ towel
5. ________ shorts
6. ________ boat
7. ________ bottle
8. ________ cloud

Numbers

Look at the pictures below. Count and write the correct number in words.

1.  ________ apples
2.  ________ birds
3.  ________ flowers
4.  ________ pencils
5.  ________ tomatoes

 ISBN 978-93-5103-599-2

Fruits and vegetables

Match each picture with a name. Underline the fruits and circle the vegetables.

1.		•	• a.	apple
2.		•	• b.	cabbage
3.		•	• c.	corn
4.		•	• d.	mango
5.		•	• e.	orange
6.		•	• f.	pineapple
7.		•	• g.	carrot
8.		•	• h.	pear
9.		•	• i.	banana
10.		•	• j.	potato

 ISBN 978-93-5103-599-2